AMAZING

FALSEHOODS

101 extraordinary pieces of disinformation

By Brandon Match

Yackety Schmack
PUBLISHING

Published by Yackety Schmack Publishing

Copyright © Brandon Match 2009

ISBN 978-0-9564393-0-7

If all the cars in Europe were arranged end-to-end, it would be possible to spell out the words 'pointless exercise' in letters 200 miles high. The cars would also contain enough coolant to poison every statistician on the planet six times over.

Neurologists attending a children's birthday party
in Whitstable discovered that a 1 litre cocktail of
lemonade, jelly and raspberry ripple ice cream
can have the same effect on an eight year old's
brain as two grams of crystal meth.

All roads used to lead to Rome, until a global programme of highway development in the mid 1970s re-routed several thousand of the world's largest carriageways. Technically, all roads now lead to Sleaford in Lincolnshire.

The first person to cross the M25 on a pogo stick was attempting to raise awareness of the issues facing one-legged kangaroos in Tasmania. The stunt went largely unnoticed, and the special needs of Tasmania's monopedal kangaroo population are still being ignored by a government that simply doesn't care.

The hiccups now kill more people each year than traffic accidents and dog attacks combined. As a result, a leading dictionary has changed part of its definition of 'hiccup' from "A slight error or brief interruption" to "A catastrophic event with enormous implications".

People who spend more than three hours a week watching soap operas double their chances of becoming clinically depressed. Conversely, people who regularly watch lambs frolicking tend to feel deliriously happy all the time.

Hull's worst ever case of cannibalism involved three generations of the same family. The youngest victim, Jo, died in his sleep in 1967 and was immediately devoured by his mother, Jill. Two days later, Jill was murdered and eaten by her father, Pat, who then suffered a fatal heart attack. The coroner described Pat's autopsy as being "Like opening up a set of Russian dolls".

Britain's most enigmatic tombstone can be found in the graveyard of Saint Margaret the Enhancer's Church, Stowe-on-the-Wold, Gloucestershire. Its inscription reads: "He died as he lived; in a big mug of tea."

In March 1997 a man from Barnsley used two metres of rubber tubing, a high powered water pump, a tranquiliser gun and a 15 year old mare called Bessy to prove that you can lead a horse to water and make it drink.

It is widely accepted that by 2050 husbands will have been rendered obsolete by the introduction of mass-produced robots specialising in DIY and spider-removal. In 2051 a global 'man versus machine' war is predicted, the outcome of which will ultimately decide the future of domestic life on Earth.

Llamas can survive for three days after decapitation, although they are likely to be shunned by the rest of the herd throughout that time. After two days of social isolation, 70% of headless Llamas attempt suicide.

The world's most expensive cheese is made from etruscan pygmy shrew milk. The product, which smells like digestive biscuits and costs £56,000 per gram, has so far only ever featured on one episode of Ready Steady Cook.

Exposure to sunshine has been proven to boost self-confidence and ambition, but impair one's ability to shave or choose a sensible hairstyle. Adolf Hitler was a keen amateur sunbather.

The giant stone heads of Easter Island are playing pieces from an ancient chess-like game called Raa Tui. Neighbouring tribes would take turns to move the huge pieces around in games that could take centuries to complete. The island and its heads were eventually abandoned 800 years ago when somebody invented Noughts and Crosses.

The tradition of waving a chequered flag at the end of a motor race began in the 17th century, when a serving wench halted a runaway pony by throwing a chessboard at its face. Racing drivers still consider it good luck to assault a horse with a board game before each race.

In California bald people can claim a $3,000 Hair Restoration Grant from the state Tourism Bureau as part of its 'Keep Cali Beautiful' campaign. In 2006 the Bureau, which also advocates enforced dental correction for those with crooked teeth, was criticised by the UN for building a chain of controversial Obesity Death Camps.

Cornish pasties are "quite nice". This was the finding of a nationwide survey of four thousand pie enthusiasts, who were asked to rate iconic pastry/meat combinations on a scale ranging from 'Sublime dinner proposition' to 'Deeply troubling crap-snack'.

On Christmas day 1988, staff at London Zoo were amazed to observe a group of captive chimpanzees playing charades. The game descended into anarchy when one chimp was spotted mouthing the word 'Emmerdale' to another player.

By 2020, economists predict that Bournemouth's elderly population will have ceased using money altogether, favouring instead a trade system based entirely on coupons, vouchers and rewards points.

Corrugated cardboard was first developed as a form of social housing for tapeworms. Unfortunately, the pressures of living in such close proximity to each other proved disastrous for the worms, and drug abuse ran rife in what quickly became cardboard ghettos.

The Armenian flag depicts two leopards cuddling each other in the presence of a bearded quantity surveyor. The scene commemorates a defining passage from the country's national book – 'Jungle love at the building site'.

Students from Cranfield University spent five years attempting to fill a test tube with pure disappointment, which they filtered out of the atmosphere during crucial Tim Henman matches at Wimbledon. They almost succeeded...

Yellow sanitation cubes, of the type commonly found in public toilets, can be used in the same way as cough sweets. Their ability to sooth oesophageal discomfort was first discovered by a Doberman Pincher called Trish, who accidentally swallowed one while drinking from a urinal in the East Midlands.

The first heart bypass was performed in 1432 by a Shepherd called Abraham Fist. The patient survived, even though Mr Fist, having no access to a scalpel, was forced to carry out the entire operation using a shovel.

Fruit bowls are receptacles for fruit. It is also a popular sport among the elderly tribespeople of Papua New Guinea, who compete to see which of them can roll pomegranates closest to a kumquat jack.

An average UK portion of fish and chips contains 106 chips, but only one fish. In 1987 the EC launched a failed attempt to rectify this disparity, by insisting that chip shop owners halve the number of chips in a portion, while increasing the number of fish to 53.

The longest human pregnancy in recorded history lasted seven years. When Tina Stott of Danton, Kentucky finally gave birth to her son, he was immediately able to walk, talk and perform many of the Jackson Five's dance routines.

In Victorian times it was considered shameful for women to eat 'phallic' foods, such as bananas, in public. If a man suspected that his wife had been seen outside the marital home with rice pudding on her chin, he was within his rights to file for divorce.

In 2007 holy men representing the major monotheistic religions attended a conference to discuss why most prayers go unanswered. Having concluded that God must be deaf, the delegates offered prayers for an improvement in His hearing.

In 1932 a Texan entrepreneur called Christopher Corn attempted to market boxes of his own dandruff as a breakfast cereal. 'Corn's Flakes' did not sell well, but the idea was seized upon by opportunistic farmers who replaced skin with corn as the central ingredient and made a fortune.

Fire eating was first attempted by starving French peasants during the 'Grande Famine' of 1032. Though low in nutritional value, flames were found to be surprisingly filling, and imbued with a subtle, smokey flavour reminiscent of kippers.

The arrangement of letters on a standard English language keyboard is a throwback to Elizabethan times, when the plague was blamed on dairy products. 'QWERTY' is an acronym of the cautionary phrase "Query What Evil Resides in Thy Yoghurt."

Research has shown that fried foods, fizzy drinks, cakes, pastries, beer, hamburgers, pizza, full fat cream, sausages, steak and chocolate are all so delicious that they can fight cancer and reduce the risk of heart disease.

Chewing gum cannot be created or destroyed. The substance originally fell to Earth 5 million years ago in one three mile wide block, fragments of which have since found their way to almost every corner of the planet. In 2076 all chewing gum will spontaneously coalesce at a location near Stockport.

Dexter Tossnugget won the Iowa State Ridiculous Name Competition a record 15 times in a row between 1978 and 1993. His reign eventually came to an end in April 1994, when a baby boy from Mason City was christened Trackshite Grease Foundation-Mask.

Crosswords are designed purely to infuriate and annoy - hence the name. The same is true of 'rage ball'; an ancient and deeply exasperating game which, for reasons long since forgotten, was renamed 'golf' in the 1700s.

Nutritionists have found that there is some truth in many of the old wives tales concerning certain foods. Carrots do improve night vision, spinach is linked to increased muscle strength, and beans have been shown to make levitation possible.

Inspired by the work of George Washington Carver, enthusiastic Welsh scientist Trefor Jones spent his entire career developing innovative uses for the onion. By the time of his death, Jones had patented over 7,000 onion-based products, ranging from motorcycles to radios. All of his inventions taste delicious when fried.

Yorkshire's claim to be 'God's own county' became a provable fact in 1998, when every acre of land in the East Riding, North, South and West Yorkshire was purchased at auction by the supreme deity. The excited new owner reportedly said that He had "big plans for the area".

Cats have a highly developed section in their brains which allows them to perform some acts of mind control. This explains why many people will happily house, medicate and feed cats, in exchange for nothing more than a flowerbed full of faeces.

When an electric current is passed through a saucer of milk, cheese accumulates around the positive electrode, and butter builds up at the negative. It is believed that early man first discovered dairy products by witnessing lightening strike a buffalo's udder.

Far from being a religious site, archaeologists now believe that Stonehenge was western Europe's first public convenience. The site's epic scale is said to reflect the importance that ancient Britons placed on an enjoyable bowel movement.

Anaemic people are around 12% more buoyant than the rest of the population because their blood contains so little iron. Conversely, those afflicted with haemochromatosis have too much iron in their bodies, making them more prone to rust.

Some species of goat can detect the presence of correction fluid on a document up to five miles away. This remarkable ability was harnessed by the Canadian government, who trained goats to hunt down and attack careless students in the 1980s.

Ear lobes are vestigial structures which serve no purpose in modern humans. Biologists believe that they may be the remains of simple flippers, which our ancient ancestors used to stabilise their heads while grazing on marine algae.

Hobson's Dysfunction is a virulent disease which grossly inflates a sufferer's sense of their own importance. In 1970 a major outbreak of Hobson's Dysfunction occurred in Australia, where it continues to influence the national psyche to this day.

Robin Hood regularly lined up key personalities from his famous guerrilla army and 'disrespected' them in front of Maid Marian. Over time this affected morale to such an extent that the team changed its name from the 'Band of Merry Men' to 'The Loose Affiliation of Embittered Forest Warriors'.

The Vatican has its own air force, made up of 15 radio controlled model aeroplanes 'piloted' by tamarin monkeys. Each plane's flight is actually controlled by a Cardinal on the ground; the tamarins' responsibility is simply to identify and then bomb non-believers.

In times of stress a male Emu will push its head up its own rectum. This trait is said to have been the inspiration for Shakespeare's famous line: "With nose twixt cheeks, he dodged the greater stench that seethed about his feet."

The first laptop computers came with a health warning because they were heavy enough to crush a child's femur. For a brief period during the 1990s, lap injuries caused by the crippling weight of portable computers were cited as the most common cause of school absenteeism in Norway.

In 1987 lab rats at the Tring Institute of Science went on strike for three weeks when it was revealed that guinea pigs in the cages opposite were given larger food rations and a much less demanding schedule of toxic injections.

The Dead Sea is so salty that any organic matter deposited in its waters will be preserved indefinitely. Some beauty-conscious Jordanian scuba divers have capitalised on this fact by spending almost their entire lives in a so-called Youth Commune on the sea floor.

The average UK office contains 8 whingers, 7 backstabbers, 2 psychopaths, 9.63 pedants and 11 gits. Together, the negative energy they produce in one week would be enough to boil 70,000 kettles.

People with blonde hair are highly resistant to fire. In the middle ages, fair-haired women found guilty of witchcraft could spend days burning at the stake, in many cases outlasting the available supply of fire wood. In such situations, they would simply be stabbed.

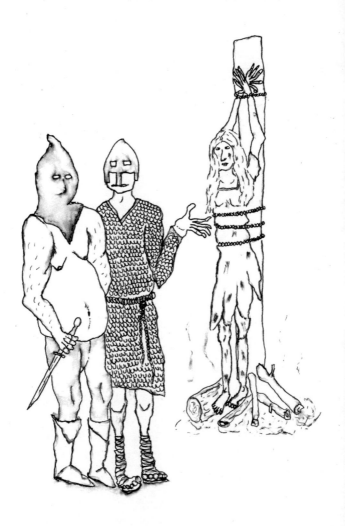

Many western countries are experiencing a 'generational ability gap', characterised by relatively low IT skill levels among the oldest people in society, and a corresponding deficit in 'traditional' skills among the young. In 2006 a study revealed that only 2 out of 7 British teenagers can operate a hammer.

13% of the world's fresh water is retained in the ankles and lower legs of pregnant women. If all of this water was bought together in one place, the volume of liquid amassed would be sufficient to wash 5.9 trillion soiled nappies.

Every seven seconds somebody in the UK will fail to catch a sausage roll that has been thrown to them by a family member. Dropping or fumbling pastry snacks is now the leading cause of embarrassment in British homes.

The world's most expensive aircraft carriers were nicknamed 'Nasty Jacks'. Built entirely of gold, they had no means of propulsion, did not float and were too small to accommodate any aircraft. Despite these drawbacks, the Ugandan navy placed an order for 500 of them in March 1976.

Militant geographer Dr Valerie Mallet gained notoriety in the 1940s for her pioneering work with mud. Over a two year period, Dr Mallet spent 3.6 million US tax dollars investigating the sexual preferences of wet soil – an endeavour which earned her the Nobel Prize for Lunacy in 1949.

Pizza was invented in West Yorkshire by a plumber called Alan Thorpe. Following almost three decades of development, Mr Thorpe's 'Edible flying disk for the energetic picnicker' was unveiled to an astonished public in May 1932.

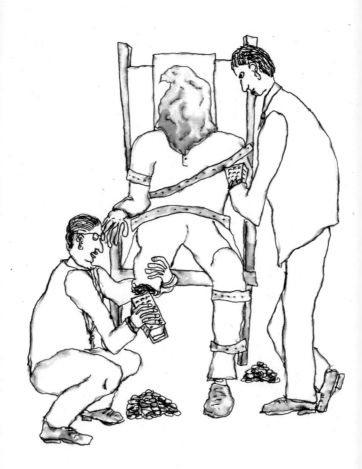

When East Dakota State Penitentiary's electric chair broke down in 1956, the prison's governor instructed executioners to continue their work using a cheese grater. Starting at the feet, it took two men an average of five hours to rasp one medium-sized convict into oblivion.

Scotland's summer midge population reached its current plague-like proportions following a rumour within the insect community that loch water is alcoholic. The rumour was quickly revealed to be false, but many midges still return each year for the scenery.

'Twelve dead squirrels in a cardboard box' is the most popular record ever released by Columbian rock star Germaine Chugnut. The song, which has sold over 38 million copies, was inspired by Chugnut's experiences on the refunds and returns counter of a Bogotá pet store.

Ancient Mongolians were able to cure chronic back pain by pelting the patient with hedgehogs. This treatment was later adopted by the Chinese, who refined it into the practice that we know today as acupuncture.

Badgers do not exist. They were a marketing ploy devised by advertising executives in the 1960s to increase sales of black and white paint. Later campaigns are responsible for similarly enduring myths, including the existence of pandas, zebras and Alistair Darling.

Current estimates put the number of flamingos in Dublin at 4.5 billion. Scientists suggest that the birds, which have been flocking to the Irish capital in increasing numbers since the early '80s, are attracted by the city's party atmosphere and wealth of traditional pubs.

In Belgium there are no laws against robbery or assault, but it is illegal to shout through a cardboard tube. So-called 'Pipe Screamers' are sent on compulsory rehabilitation courses, and encouraged to take up more socially acceptable pastimes, such as smoking crack.

Property prices in South East England have been rising year-on-year for the past 17 centuries. In 305AD the average cost of a studio mud hut in the region was around one and a half bags of pig's teeth. Today, the same property could cost in excess of £3.2 million.

For a brief period during the 1880s, the number 25 was phased out due to lack of demand. It was eventually reinstated following the enormous success of a music hall song called 'My heart's in slightly more than two dozen pieces over you.'

Fork-lift truck enthusiast Sheik Al Qadur commissioned the world's first Spoon-lift truck in 1983. A prototype Knife-lift truck followed two years later. All three vehicles were used in an ill-fated attempt to feed an adult bull elephant at a gigantic dinner table in 1986.

The Harvard Cuteness Index (HCI) lists 15,000 organisms in order of how loveable they are. Young mammals dominate the top portion of the list, with various types of mould occupying the lower places. Predictably, those species of mould which develop a furry covering rank slightly higher than those which do not.

Scientists testing the hypothesis that "All work and no play makes Jack a dull boy" found that their subject, 8 year old Jack Rawson of Coventry, actually became shinier after toiling non-stop in a field for three months.

Eccentric circus owner Frazer Tats famously drove everywhere in a chariot pulled by alligators, until ill health forced him to trade the vehicle in for a 1 litre Nissan Micra. Tats' last words were reported to be: "Ain't nobody gonna tell me that exhaust fumes smell sweeter than 'gator fart".

The contradictory beliefs of people who wear leather shoes but refuse to eat meat can be traced back to Rita Westangle, a radical vegetarian who claimed to have had telepathic conversations with cows that "abhorred gluttony, but would happily die for fashion".

The most successful synchronised swimmer of all time was Phyllis Garside, a district nurse from Grimbsy, East Yorkshire. The five times world champion was forced to retire from the sport in 1982 having mislaid her goggles.

Ironically, the term 'politically correct' was first used to describe any woman whose waist measurement fell within the required limits for her to be allowed to serve tea in the House of Commons.

Because the term 'Road Rage' is now so closely associated with angry drivers, psychologists have had to devise a new name for the phenomenon of outraged roads. In 2007 they settled on 'Furious Highway Syndrome'.

The sport of tenpin bowling has its roots in a ceremonial rite of passage undertaken by adolescent Swiss boys. In order to prove that they had become men, participants would stand motionless on the side of an Alp while village elders rolled two ton balls of cheese directly at them.

Prior to 1922 swearing did not exist in the English language. All the words we currently consider to be offensive were picked at random from the dictionary and assigned their new vulgar status by a self-appointed panel of bored housewives called The Seekers of Outrage.

The word 'broccoli' comes from the French verb 'broquolir', which means "To cause disgust or revulsion; to incite to vomit." Oscar Wilde once described broccoli as "cauliflower that failed its eleven plus".

In Australia, drinking beer and then driving is only considered criminal if the beer was warm at the time of its consumption. If found guilty, motorists must regurgitate, refrigerate and then re-drink the contents of their stomachs.

Nasal hair is twice as strong as steel, and ear hair is three times more elastic than rubber. Armpit hair is relatively weak and inelastic, but it can withstand huge extremes of temperature. A composite twine woven from all three hair types is currently being tested at NASA.

It would cost an estimated £900,000 to repaint every elongated bicycle on the UK's cycle paths. According to the action group Circus Performers Against Excessive Council Tax, the price of undertaking such a task could be slashed by 50% if unicycles were the norm.

On 23 May 1925 a Cheshire woman gave birth to identical female triplets, and a fourth child whose body was composed entirely of coal. The triplets all lived to 63 years of age and are buried in Chester cathedral. The coal boy died aged 65 and was cremated.

83% of the world's amusingly-shaped root vegetables are grown in farmland belonging to a Mr Chag Hackson of Gwent, Illinois. Ironically, Mr Hackson first achieved notoriety during the 1950s as part of a travelling freak show, where he performed as 'The man whose penis looks like a potato'.

Children who are brought up in close proximity to electricity pylons are three times more likely to enjoy progressive jazz music than healthy children of the same age.

In order to travel a distance of fifteen meters, a giant African land snail must secrete the same amount of mucus as one person with influenza produces in a week. If a giant African land snail were to catch flu, one of its sneezes could fill an Olympic swimming pool.

Rhinoceros horns are formed by the gradual accumulation of salts, which are deposited when the mammal's tears evaporate. The size of a rhino's horn depends entirely on the beast's age and emotional disposition.

Onutrimania is an insatiable craving for bright orange foods. People with the condition have been known to bankrupt themselves by stockpiling enormous quantities of carrots, oranges and cheap supermarket-brand fish fingers.

Cod liver oil is actually a thin wax, extracted from the ears of mice by means of a special 'hat'. The oil has absolutely no health benefits for humans, yet its production is responsible for the humiliation of 4.6 billion rodents every year.

The dimensions of office paper were standardised by a Dutch printer called Baston Gallery. Inspired by his love of the natural world, Gallery used the depth of a sperm whale's blow hole to determine the length of a page, and the wingspan of a budgerigar to set the width. 'A4' stands for A-mazing Fau-na.

Psychologists investigating the relationship between small talk and brain function have found that women are five times more resistant to the harmful effects of tittle-tattle than men are. Attendance at just one coffee morning can be enough to induce coma in an otherwise healthy adult male.

In 1963 a panel of 15 linguistic scholars met at Potsdam to try and solve "The biggest mystery in the English language". After three months of intense discussion, the group was no closer to explaining why so many people insist on pronouncing the word 'skeleton' as 'skelington'.

In 2009 half of all UK suicides were committed by people who could no longer cope with the volume of junk mail entering their homes. At one shared house in Manchester, six residents were found dead next to a vast suicide note, made from over 2,500 fast food flyers. The note simply said: "None of us even like pizza."

By an incredible coincidence, the first person in the world to be fitted with a prosthetic lower limb was a woman called Faye Clegg. The first electronically controlled prosthetic upper limb was grafted on to a man called Rob Oticarm.

One in seven unopened sardine tins contains a fish which is still alive. Though easily revived by immersion in a bowl of cold water, such fish often carry serious emotional scars from their time in the can, and so make very poor pets.

Lake Baikal in Siberia is home to a species of aquatic rabbit found nowhere else on Earth. With webbed feet, a streamlined body and nostrils that have migrated to the tips of its ears, the creature is perfectly adapted for 'snorkeling' near the lake shore in search of sunken carrots.

Over the course of a lifetime, the average British person will spend a total of nine weeks searching their home for the source of unexplained buzzing sounds. According to mental health experts, unidentifiable humming or buzzing noises are a major contributing factor in 87% of nervous breakdowns.

The width of a milkman's thumb is directly proportional to the volume of yoghurt he can sell in one year. Female milkmen - or 'milknymphs' - will generally sell more cream on the fifth day of their menstrual cycles.

In 2005 atheistic French sculptor Jacques T Charliot produced a highly controversial piece entitled 'Spread the word'. Described by Charliot as "a comment on the veracity of religious teachings", the work consisted of a butter knife and two pieces of dog excrement, displayed next to a toasted crumpet.

Spending hours on end inventing statements which have no basis in fact can induce a kind of delirium, in which the lie-writer begins to question the nature of reality. Fish swim backwards when they are depressed.